Piano · Vocal · Guitar

TOP COUNTRY HITS '02

S0-AJW-615

CONTENTS

ISBN 0-634-04485-0

HAL•LEONARD®
CORPORATION
7777 W. BLUEMOUND RD. P.O. BOX 13819 MILWAUKEE, WI 53213

Visit Hal Leonard Online at
www.halleonard.com

ANGELS IN WAITING

Words and Music by STEWART HARRIS,
JIM McBRIDE and TAMMY COCHRAN

We camped out on the liv-ing room floor,___ in our
They al-ways knew they'd___ nev-er grow old.___

old sleep-in' bags___ by a make-be-lieve fire.___ In a___ tent made of cov-ers
Some-times the bod-y is___ weak-er than___ the soul. In their dark-est hour___

we talked for hours,___ my two broth-ers and me.
I made a prom-ise I will al-ways___ keep.___

Original key: F♯ major. This edition has been transposed up one half-step to be more playable.

ANGRY ALL THE TIME

Words and Music by
BRUCE ROBISON

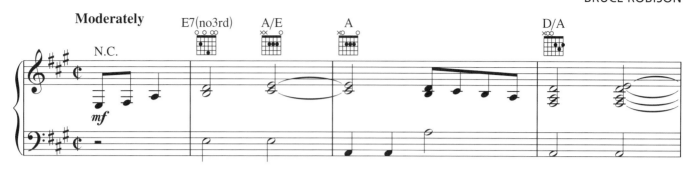

Here we are, _____ what is left _____ of a hus-

-band and ___ a wife with four good kids ___ who

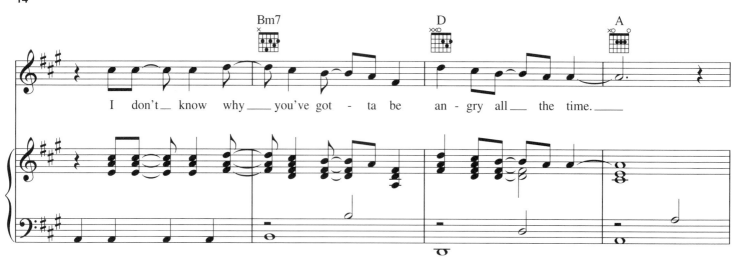

I don't know why ___ you've got - ta be an - gry all ___ the time. ___

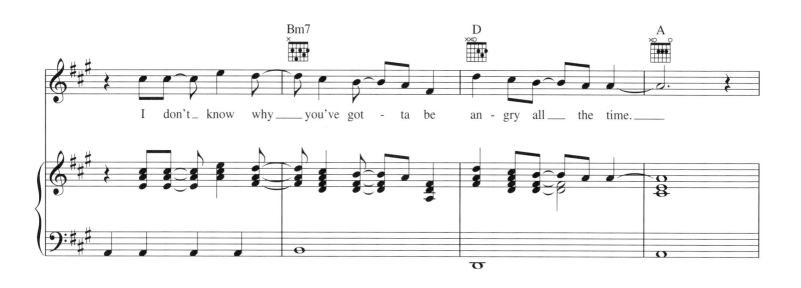

I don't know why ___ you've got - ta be an - gry all ___ the time. ___

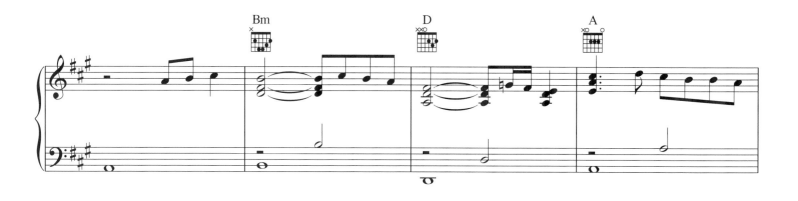

rit.

BLESSED

Words and Music by BRETT JAMES,
HILLARY LINDSEY and TROY VERGES

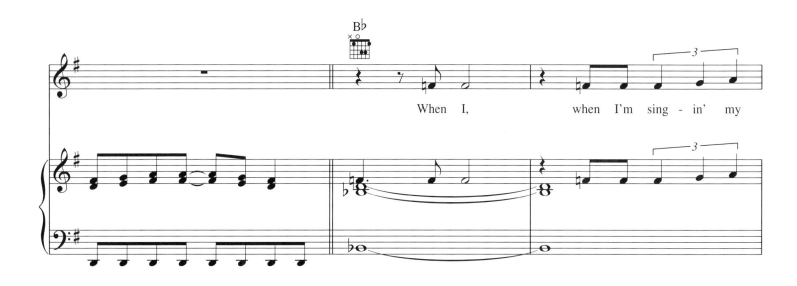

When I,   when I'm sing - in' my

kids to sleep, ___   when I feel you hold - in' me, _____

BRING ON THE RAIN

Words and Music by BILLY MONTANA
and HELEN DARLING

I WANNA TALK ABOUT ME

Words and Music by
BOBBY BRADDOCK

Moderately fast

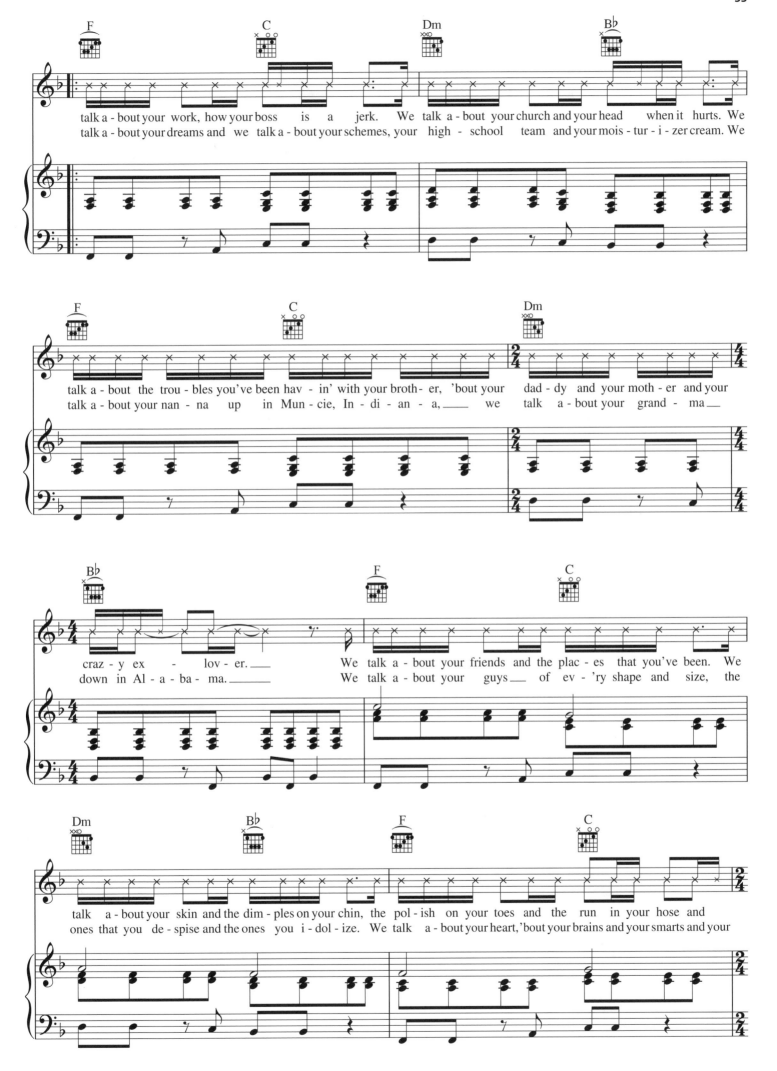

I WOULD'VE LOVED YOU ANYWAY

Words and Music by MARY DANNA
and TROY VERGES

I'M ALREADY THERE

Words and Music by RICHIE McDONALD,
FRANK MYERS and GARY BAKER

I'M JUST TALKIN' ABOUT TONIGHT

Words and Music by SCOTTY EMERICK
and TOBY KEITH

WHEN GOD-FEARIN' WOMEN GET THE BLUES

Words and Music by
LESLIE SATCHER

Slow and freely

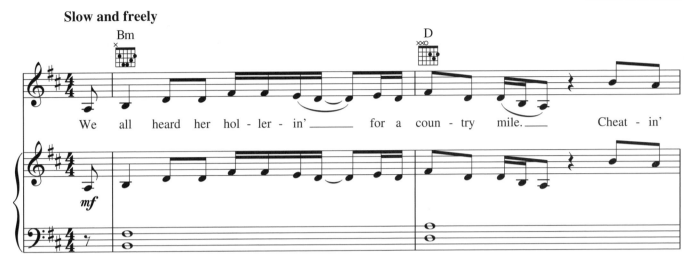

We all heard her hol-er-in' _____ for a coun-try mile. _____ Cheat-in'

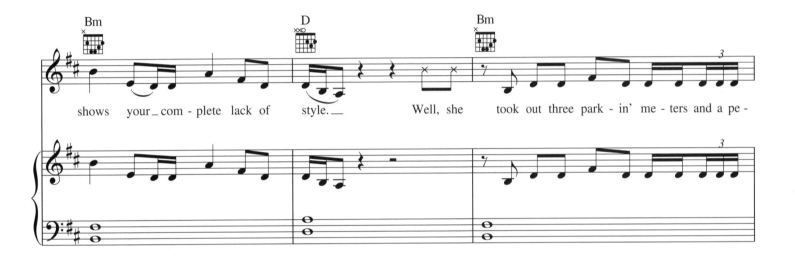

shows your _ com-plete lack of style. _____ Well, she took out three park-in' me-ters and a pe-

des-tri-an's purse the day she quit the Bap-tist choir and threw that Ford in-to re-

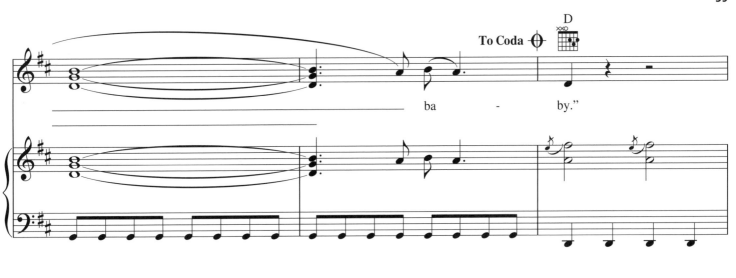

To Coda ⊕ D

ba - by."

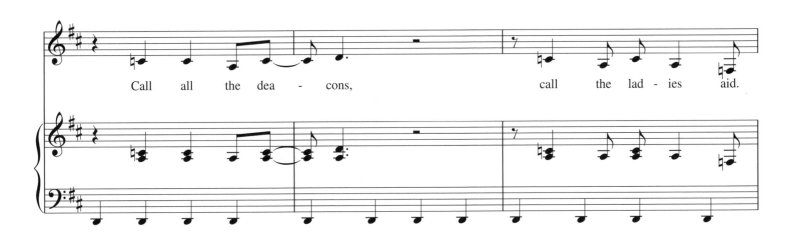

Call all the dea - cons, call the lad - ies aid.

Call all the ___ al - tos, sop - ran - os,

Slow and freely

She's on all our prayer lists, she's on all our hearts. As for the Eas - ter Can - ta - ta, we don't

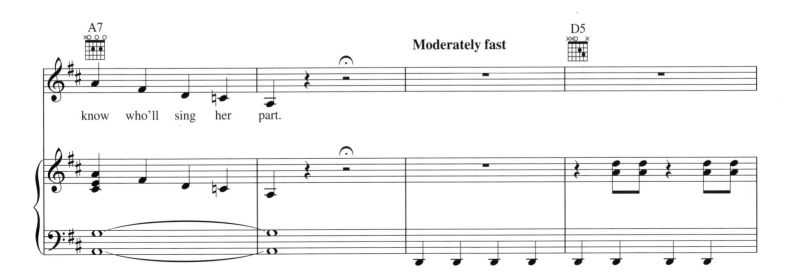

know who'll sing her part.

batch of grav - y. You don't have to be____ my ____
(be my, be my,) ____

____ ba - by."

Repeat and Fade   **Optional Ending**

I'M TRYIN'

Words and Music by ANTHONY SMITH,
CHRIS WALLIN and JEFFREY STEELE

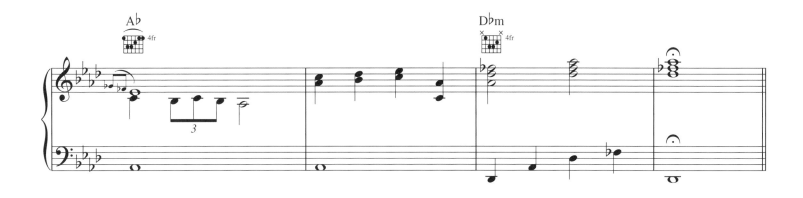

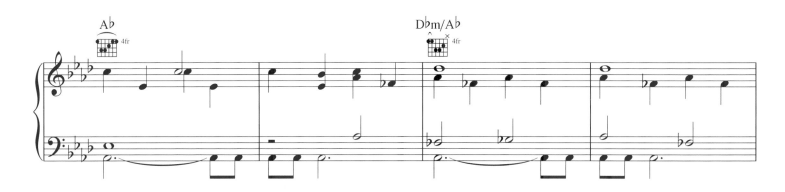

IT'S A GREAT DAY TO BE ALIVE

Words and Music by
DARRELL SCOTT

Ow - ooh _____

ONLY IN AMERICA

Words and Music by KIX BROOKS,
DON COOK and RONNIE ROGERS

Moderately fast

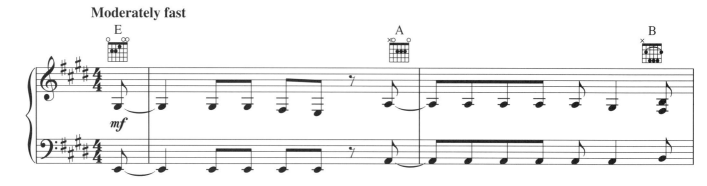

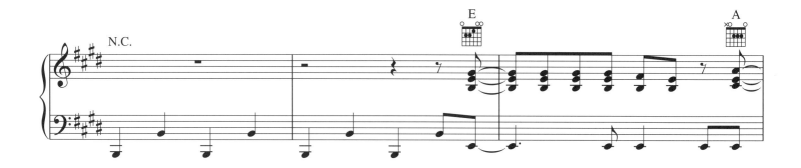

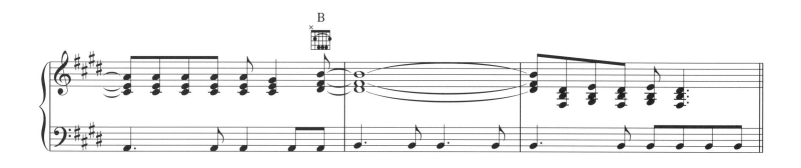

Sun com - in' up   o - ver New York Cit - y.

Sun go - in' down   on an L. A. free - way,

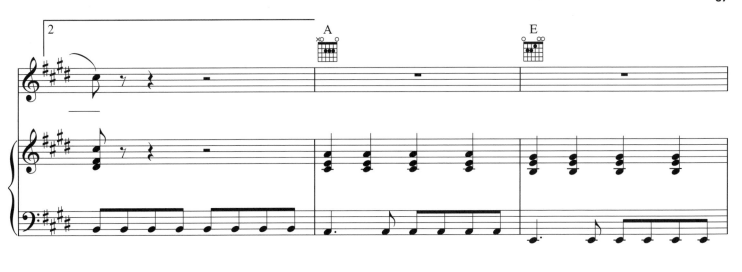

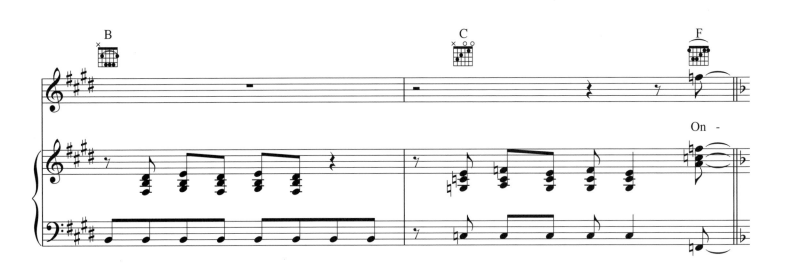

On -

RUN

Words and Music by ANTHONY SMITH
and TONY LANE

Moderately slow

TWO PEOPLE FELL IN LOVE

Words and Music by BRAD PAISLEY,
TIM OWENS and KELLEY LOVELACE

Moderately

WHAT I REALLY MEANT TO SAY

Words and Music by CYNDI THOMSON,
CHRIS WATERS and TOMMY LEE JAMES

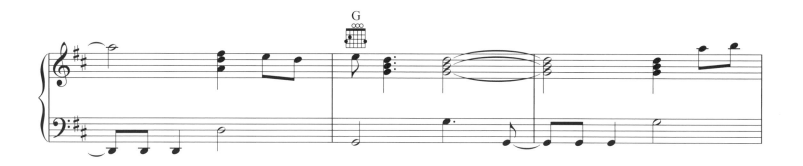

Original key: D♭ major. This edition has been transposed up one half-step to be more playable.

WHEN I THINK ABOUT ANGELS

Words and Music by JAMIE O'NEAL,
ROXIE DEAN and SONNY TILLIS

WHERE THE STARS AND STRIPES AND THE EAGLE FLY

Words and Music by AARON TIPPIN,
CASEY BEATHARD and KENNY BEARD

Well, if you ask me, where I ___ come from, here's what I ___ tell ev - 'ry - one. ___

WHERE WERE YOU
(When the World Stopped Turning)

Words and Music by
ALAN JACKSON

WHO I AM

Words and Music by BRETT JAMES
and TROY VERGES

WITH ME

Words and Music by BRETT JAMES
and TROY VERGES

Moderately fast

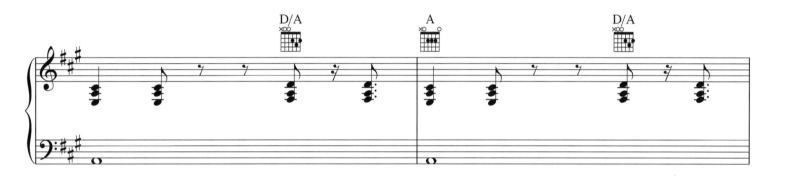

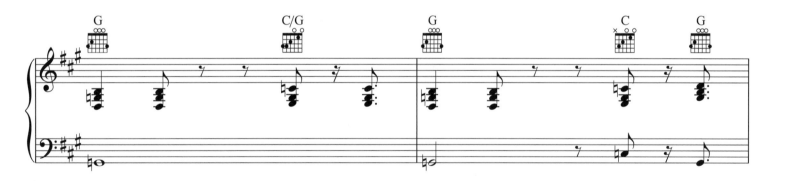

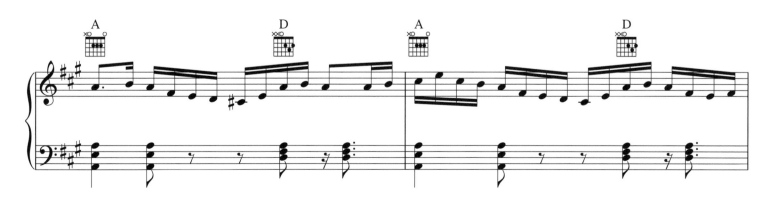

WITHOUT YOU

Words and Music by NATALIE MAINES
and ERIC SILVER

WRAPPED AROUND

Words and Music by BRAD PAISLEY,
CHRIS DuBOIS and KELLEY LOVELACE

Yes sir,___ I love her ver - y much. I know it's on - ly been sev - en months.___